The Razor's Edge of Teaching

The Razor's Edge of Teaching

John Glennon

Kai'koa Books

Hilo

Kai'koa Books First Edition 2010

ISBN 978-0-578-04280-0

Kai'koa Books
1592 Kilauea Ave.
Hilo, HI 96720

Contents

Contents

A Note on Sources

Although the readings and comments have been presented in my own words and style, many of their inspirations have come from the titles listed in ***Sources***. Credited quotations I gathered over the years in my journals. Their sources may not always be identified or correctly identified. I apologize to all those who are not credited and will include those citations in future editions when informed of them.

Preface

A peasant was walking back from his field when a tiger chased him to a cliff. To avoid being devoured, the peasant swung himself over the cliff's edge by holding onto a short vine. However, just as his left hand was sliding down the vine, the tiger's fangs snatched it off. Now, as the peasant struggled to hold on with his remaining hand, two mice—one black and one white—poked their heads out from the rocks and began to nibble away at the vine. At this point, the peasant noticed a wild strawberry plant growing out of the cliff face. And on that plant was a luscious strawberry. The peasant looked up into the tiger's maw and felt the vine giving way. He let go, plucked the bright red fruit, and remarked:

"What a wonderful strawberry."

Comment: What you're holding in your hands is *not* a nuts and bolts manual for writing better lesson plans. You might be wondering, then, why read this little book? Good question. Try this: Let go.

One of these pages might be your strawberry.

A Way to Read This Book

One evening a master was called into the room of a disciple. A single candle illumined the disciple's face and a notebook on the table. The disciple looked up from his notes on the master's teachings and confessed that after all his years of studying he still hadn't found his way into enlightenment. The master smiled, blew out the candle, and set him free.

Comment: You will find after each reading a comment. The comment is not necessary for understanding the connection between the reading and teaching. As a matter of fact, the comment is superfluous. Think of it this way. The reading is the moon. The comment is only a finger pointing to the moon.

The readings can be read in any order. In fact, that might be the best way. Try it now. Flip open to a page and read what is there. Alan Watts, the wise teacher of Zen philosophy, referred to this as awakening through "marvelous accidents." But what if you do not find anything "marvelous" in the reading?

Blow out the candle.

The Razor's Edge

of

Teaching

The sage is an edge that doesn't cut.

Lao-Tzu

Who Are You?

A busy market square in India. A great holy man is preaching to a gathered crowd of rich and poor. Suddenly he falls silent and sits down in the dust. The crowd pushes forward and asks if anything is wrong. He replies: "To whom am I preaching? Everywhere I look, I see the face of my god."

*****

And God saw everything that he had made and, behold, it was very good.

Genesis 1.32

Comment: One afternoon, Buddha was strolling in the cool of creation when he came upon a freshly opened violet. He delightedly exclaimed: "Ah, there I am."

Master teachers try to find—if not a god—then a god-like goodness in all things. On some days it may be hard to recognize in the face of a sullen student something other than rebellion. Our intellectual anger begins to smolder on the kindling of impatience. At that moment, we might try saying to ourselves:

Who Are You?

"Ah, there I am." It may help calm the moment and put into perspective who we are.

See also

Butcher

Dharma Bum Prayer

Wisdom

Disciple: What is wisdom?

Sage: Mistake, mistake, mistake.

Comment: Shunryu Suzuki reminds us that "just to live is to live in problems." Master teachers greet each student mistake or problem with a half-smile. They humbly acknowledge the "charm of incompleteness" in both their students and themselves. The old poet in Roberto Bolaño's novel *The Savage Detectives* says, "What we now call problems, in our youth we called surprises." That would be an interesting way of looking at a classroom of frustrated students. Not as problems, but as surprises.

In other words: Nobody is perfect. In other words: The world is perfect.

See also

Paradox

Wash Your Plate

Is That So?

One day the King's chamberlain marched into the royal kitchen and exclaimed, "The King has fallen ill." The cook said, "Is that so?" The chamberlain added, "And the royal doctors have concluded the fault is to be found in your cooking. Pack up. You're fired." The cook said, "Is that so?"

Years later, the chamberlain came upon the cook begging in a village. The homeless cook was dressed in rags and appeared emaciated. When the chamberlain dropped a coin in his outstretched hand, the cook looked up and gave him a toothless grin of recognition. As much as the chamberlain didn't want to admit it, he confessed that soon after the cook was let go the real source of the King's illness had been determined. "A flea bite," the chamberlain uncomfortably chuckled. "And to think, all these years you were innocent."

"Is that so?" the cook said.

Comment: The way of teaching can be fraught with accolades and accusations. Students, parents, administrators, school board members and colleagues stand before us in poses of applause or rebuke. There are even days when we stand before ourselves in admiration or reproach from one teaching period to the next. How should we respond to these judgments? At times it might be difficult to accept that once the praise or blame (whether deserved or not) has been given, it becomes a reality. It becomes *just so.* But whatever is just so today will be some other just so tomorrow.

"Vanity of vanities, said the preacher, vanity of vanities; all is vanity." Koheleth, the wise preacher in Ecclesiastes, implies that we should not be overly concerned with the day's judgments. "Vanity" in the context of his philosophy means "emptiness," like the wind. Teaching reputation is a vanity—a striving after wind.

Now, take a master teacher who is lauded for an excellent examination score in the morning and rebuked for a poor coaching call in the evening. What do you suppose this master teacher's reply will be to each judgment?

See also

Smiling Beggar

Paradox

Water Teaching

The great ocean governs all bodies of water because it is beneath them.

Lao-Tzu

Comment: Other sages add to Lao-Tzu's insight that a great ocean also accepts all kinds of water—polluted or clean, rushing or sluggish. Master teachers are like a great ocean. Their students always feel welcome, no matter how long it takes to get there in terms of learning. Furthermore, master teachers do not differentiate themselves from the others flowing to them. This is not to say that teachers should be "hip" to everything in the world of students and behave as such. It does suggest that they should not belittle students to maintain their own superior intellectual position.

Water does not quarrel. When water meets a boulder, what does it do? Flows around it. And so hard is shaped by soft. Students can be hard. Some days they feel unhappy, angry, or ignorant. Master teachers flow around these feelings. Without quarreling with the student's emotions, they simply keep on teaching, knowing the student will be shaped over time. Water is patient. Master teachers are too.

Water Teaching

Each day master teachers cultivate the wisdom of patience, the humility of knowledge, and the impartiality of great oceans. That is why students flow to them.

See also

Greatest Swordsman

Beggar's Wish

Wash Your Plate

For twenty years the disciple had followed his master. One day he sadly confessed, "Master, I have listened to your teachings for all these years, but I am no closer to understanding. I'm a failure." The master replied, "Is that so? Let me ask you this. What have you just done?" The disciple answered: "I have just finished my meal." The master snapped:

"Wash your plate."

Comment: A student is on the verge of tears from a low test score. The lesson is about to begin. Tears make for poor learners. Quick, what's to be done? We are on the razor's edge of teaching. In the old days, the teacher might have knuckled the student on the head for not being tough enough. Not recommended today. Try this advice. The test was yesterday; the mark was yesterday; but we are here today. Wash your plate.

The above advice can be coupled with the words of Hamlet's own awakening. After all his fretting over "to be or not to be," he concluded: "Let be. The readiness is all." Quite frankly, what else can a student do? If he is to be true to the next test, he will *be ready.*

Wash Your Plate

That is all. And once that test has passed, he must *let be*. At first, this advice may seem rather too philosophical for students, but you might be surprised at how many are re-awakened to learning by the simple notion: Wash your plate.

See also

Why Teach?

Happy

Smiling Beggar

A **smiling beggar** haunted villages up and down the countryside. Over his shoulder he carried a sack holding all his worldly possessions. From this sack, he would hand out wild berries to the village children; and in return, if he were fortunate, the parents would thank him with a handful of rice. There were days he went hungry. One afternoon, an officious village head demanded of the beggar what his goal was. The beggar smiled, dropped the sack to the ground and sat on it. The village head then demanded how the beggar would attain this goal. The beggar jumped up, swung the sack over his shoulder and walked away.

Comment: The New Testament points the way for the faithful: "Thy kingdom come, thy will be done." For Christians, heaven happens here and now when God's commandments are lived here and now. The beggar's actions point to something similar. His doing is the goal. That is where the smile is found.

So…teachers are beggars? Master teachers humbly accept this.

Smiling Beggar

Each day is about giving and taking, and many days are more about giving. Days are just so. Master teachers do not separate the goal from the journey. Each moment is a teaching moment. And in each teaching moment the smile can be found. Dogen-zenji, the great master of Shunryu Suzuki, would remind his students what the real goal is in sitting meditation: "Success or failure is not the point. Peacefulness is."

The same can be said for teaching.

See also

Is That So?

Why Teach?

Kitchen Cat

Early one morning in a remote monastery, two monks were arguing over what to feed the kitchen cat. At that point, their master walked in, picked up a meat cleaver and grabbed the cat. "I will cut this cat in half," he challenged, "unless you say one good word to save it." The monks stared at him in open-mouthed disbelief. The master promptly chopped the cat in half. Later that afternoon, the master was relating this incident to the monastery cook. Upon hearing the challenge, the cook slipped off his sandals, placed them on his head, and walked out the back door. The master smiled and said, "If only he had been there to save the cat."

Comment: Please don't call the animal protection agency on this strict master. These ancient wisdom stories are symbolic utterances meant to shake up our everyday way of thinking. Here is one way to read this story from a teaching point of view. The cat is the student. The argument over what to feed the cat is one of teaching methodology. When the lesson plan begins to wobble, the good word symbolizes that teaching moment of success or failure. Of course, the real master here is the monastery cook. His spontaneous and unorthodox answer would have saved the cat. He walks out on the question and into life. How many times have we been put on this razor's edge of teaching? A class struggles to grasp how to solve a differential equation or unexpectedly enquires into the "why" of reading *As I Lay Dying*. Quick now—what's the good word? In an instant, master teachers "put sandals on their heads," walk out of the lesson plan, and save the class.

See also

First Lesson

Bucket of Water

Butcher

It was her husband's birthday. The mother wanted everything to be right, especially the dinner. Handing the meager kitchen savings to her son, she sent him off with this advice: "When you get to that wily butcher, tell him you want the best piece of meat he's got." Soon after, the shop's bell jingled and the boy strode up to the display case. Hoping his voice wouldn't quaver, he demanded: "Butcher, give me the best piece of meat you've got." The butcher spread his arms over the display case and replied: "They're all the best." In that instant the boy awakened.

Comment: Thirty students at their desks. Ask a teacher to pick out the best, and the finger will point to one here, one there, and—oh, yeah—maybe that one in the back. Interesting, that word *maybe.* How can the best be a *maybe*? And if that one in back is a *maybe*, then the remaining twenty-seven should be *maybe's*-- right? We are, after all, *maybe's* to one degree or another in life.

Ask master teachers who is the best, and they will point to the first student with the comment: "Not this one." And then to the second: "Not this one." And so on throughout the room. How can they be so negative? And how can their rooms be full of only poor students? They are not and they are not.

These masters simply possess the butcher's wisdom. The just so of hamburger is hamburger, not liver; therefore, hamburger is the best. The just so of pork chop is pork chop, not steak; therefore, pork chop is the best. The master teacher is pointing out the just so of Jane is Jane, not Bill—and so on. Jane is not better than Bill. How could she be? She is Jane: He is Bill. Neither is the better. Both are the best. Wouldn't it be wonderful if we could teach a room full of students who are all the best?

According to the butcher, we do.

See also

Who Am I?

Who Are You?

Greatest Swordsman

A young man swaggered up to the old master swordsman and challenged: Your sword is no longer the sharpest. I must dethrone you in combat." The old master said with a half-smile: "I am sure your sword is sharper than mine. But before proving your great skill, may I propose a preliminary contest?" Out of respect for his elder, the young man agreed, trying to hide his exasperation at this delay. The master suggested that one after the other stick his sword in the nearby stream. A leaf would then be dropped in the current, float down, and meet the sword's edge. Whichever sword cleanly cut the leaf in half would be declared the winner. "No need for bloodshed," concluded the old master. "The loser simply goes away."

The young man insisted he be tested first. He plunged his sword into the stream's muddy bottom. Down drifted the leaf, and the sword's glinting edge smoothly sliced the leaf into perfect halves. Grinning with victory, the young man crowed: "Master, you have lost. Go away." The master bowed and said with a half-smile: "Is that so? But first we must let the contest fulfill itself." In went the master's sword. Down drifted the leaf…and just as it reached the sword's edge, the leaf hesitated, slowly rotated and floated around the blade. Upon witnessing this, the young swordsman humbly bowed and said, "Master, I am not here."

Greatest Swordsman

The old master replied, "I never was."

Comment: Master teachers possess a sharp edge of knowledge, but this knowledge never cuts. It joins. Sometimes we are confronted by sharp words inside or outside the classroom: a student is upset with a grade; a colleague is unintentionally hurt by a suggestion; an administrator tables a complaint against us. Swords are drawn. Our first response might be to thrust and cut with words. But master teachers hesitate.

Yvonne Rand, a Zen Buddhist priest, suggests this way of responding: Lift the corners of your mouth in a half-smile for one… two… three…breaths. During these three, calming breaths, a spaciousness develops that might allow for a greater awareness of the argument's dimensions and possible resolutions.

Master teachers look into the faces of their antagonists and remind themselves: *Ah, there I am.* Why would they argue with themselves? They understand that winning the argument is not the purpose of being here. Peace is. Where there is peace, there is no "here" for the argument.

Greatest Swordsman

See also

A Man, a Horse, a Rope

Water Teaching

Miracles

A famous sage had his teaching interrupted by a young man at the fringe of the crowd. "Why should I believe anything you say?" the young man shouted. "My teacher works great miracles to prove the truth and power of his words. He has shot a quiver of arrows across a valley and hit the bull's-eye every time. He has thrown himself into a snake pit and emerged unharmed. He has even levitated himself above the tallest trees to manifest his wisdom."

The sage reflected for a moment and then replied: "I, too, work great miracles. At dawn, I wake. At noon, I eat. At night, I sleep."

Comment: Hand a paper clip to each student and ask how many things can be done with it. One or two will come up with a lengthy list of playful ideas. (We can only hope they become teachers, right?) For most people, a paper clip is not a miraculous object.

Master teachers, however, find the extraordinary in the ordinary. In that sense, these teachers are a bit like poets: they look at one thing and see another. Sometimes our teaching resources are, shall we say, less than adequate. That is when the sage's list reminds us of the

Miracles

miracles out there. Take Walt Whitman in his classroom of summer grass—a "uniform hieroglyphic" just waiting to be translated into wisdom.

Master teachers look out the window. There is today's lesson.

They look into a student's heart. There is another.

See also

Bucket of Water

Most Valuable Thing in the World

Boning Knife

*I***n an ancient land,** there was a sage who would point his finger to the sky to emphasize an important moment in his teaching. One morning this wise master witnessed a youthful disciple also teaching by pointing a finger to the sky. He called the young man over and politely asked him to demonstrate an effective way of imparting wisdom. The disciple grinned proudly and raised one finger to the sky. The sage seized the hand and cut the finger off with a boning knife. The young man reeled away, clutching his bloody hand. When the sage called out to the retreating disciple, the terrified youth turned to face him.

He saw one finger pointing to the sky. In that instant, he was awakened.

Comment: The unsettling teaching secret for new teachers is…there is no secret. All the classes in teaching methodology and in-service workshops will not make a master teacher. But it is surely documented that these strategies will make for better lesson plans, right? Beware the master's boning knife. Do not confuse the lesson plan with the lesson knowledge. A finger pointing to the moon is not the moon. The hard fact for new teachers to accept is that master teachers are just so.

Boning Knife

They teach from within themselves, not through others. So the next time we meet presenters on the path of in-service workshops, we will listen politely, take our notes, and congratulate them on their successes. But beware the master's boning knife. Their way can never be our way.

See also

Greetings

Bucket of Water

Gravy

I **wake up** in the morning and the rest is gravy.

Robert Frost, Nobel Laureate poet

Comment: Say a student is feeling worse than a failure. It could be anything—a missed goal, a low score on a term paper, a lost love. It sometimes helps to reassure: "Life is a miracle. You are a miracle. The rest is gravy."

See also

Happy

Wash Your Plate

Who Am I?

One day a young warrior approached the greatest master swordsman in the country and begged to be taken on as his apprentice. The master agreed, but only under one condition. “What might that be?” asked the youth. “Let me see your hands,” the master requested. The young man held out his hands for inspection. In one deft stroke the master cut them off.

The youth, fortunately, did not die. But upon full recovery he confronted the master swordsman and demanded employment in return for the irreparable damage done to him. The master agreed and made him an apprentice to the groundskeeper.

Years passed and the day arrived when the great master had to pass his sword to the next generation. All his disciples gathered in excited anticipation to hear who among them would be the Chosen One. Their master’s eyes swept the crowd, measuring the skill, grace and stamina of each of his former pupils. Finally, he raised his sword and declared: “Here is the one.”

The sword swung about and pointed to an old man washing kitchen windows with rags wrapped around stumps for hands.

Who Am I?

Comment: The master swordsman knows what makes him great: he can look out a clear window. He can act because others act. And what about the handless apprentice? Did he resent his life of service instead of swordsmanship? No. The Judeo-Christian Bible reminds us: "Those that wait upon the Lord, they shall inherit the earth." Buddha collapses the concept even further: "Who am I, if not the other?"

What if the master swordsman had continued to cut away at the youth? "What?" we exclaim in horror. Okay, try it this way. The master swordsman asks the youth: "What if I cut off your hands? Will you still be you?" "Of course," replies the youth. "And your arms?" "Of course." And so on, until just before hypothetically cutting off the youth's head, the master says, "Let's begin again. What if I first cut off your air? Will you still be you?" After a moment's thought, the youth replies, "I guess not. I'd be dead." "Just so," agrees the master. "Yet, isn't it curious we think that air is not a part of us in the same way we do our hands, heart and head.

The foreground and background are one. Master teachers appreciate this wisdom. Wisdom and peace in a student depends not only upon the teacher but also upon the superintendant, principal, secretary, and

Who Am I?

janitor. And what about the guy flipping burgers down the street? How about Miles Davis? Or water over a pebble? Imagine making a list of everything that makes up the "body" of a student. Where would it end?

The Zenrin states: "Scoop up the water and the moon is in your hands." If the student is the moon, we must be ready to hold the water.

See also

River's Secret

Miracles

Wedding Gift

She was the most beautiful lady in all of kingdom, and it didn't hurt that she was also the daughter of the king. Every eligible bachelor tried to win her scarf at the jousts and sought her hand at the balls. All to no avail. She had already found the man of her dreams--the young court painter. He had been commissioned to paint a mural for the old king's birthday.

Each morning the painter would enter the great hall, and behind a large arras, work on his creation out of sight of the court's official comings and goings. And then it happened, as so it should. In the failing light of an early autumn afternoon, the princess presented herself before the young painter just as he reappeared from behind the arras. Although he was not suitable for the blood of royalty, she boldly declared her undying love for him and voiced her wish that he should do the same for her. If you had been at the other end of the long hall, you would have seen his reply in the form of a passionate embrace and an undying kiss.

Unfortunately, the one who did see the kiss was the nobleman the king had already chosen for his daughter. The jealous nobleman ran to report the scandalous incident to his king. The old king's anger was royally magnificent. "If our daughter is hot blooded," he raged, "then

Wedding Gift

hot blood she shall have." He commanded the jealous suitor thusly: "At the moment of the unveiling of our royal gift, step up to this impudent painter and behead him with our royal sword."

The day of the birthday arrived with all the spectacle royalty can marshal to celebrate itself. The king placed his daughter next to the painter for the unveiling. The jealous nobleman placed himself behind the painter and readied the royal sword. The painter pulled the velvet rope, the arras fell, and the court gasped in astonishment. They and their king had never seen such a beautiful creation. A pastoral path led into hushing stands of pines, past rushing streams, through golden meadows, before disappearing into snow-capped peaks. All but one in the audience was enthralled, and that jealous one swung the royal sword in execution.

At that same moment, the painter took the hand of his beautiful princess, and together they stepped onto the pastoral path and walked joyously into the mountains.

Wedding Gift

Comment: Master teachers, like the court painter, recognize the importance of embodying the concept of becoming one with the knowledge. Paulo Fraire, a Brazilian educator, advises we should read the words *and* the world. Just as a mural is a representation of the world, words are a representation of reality. Rather than having our eyes walking across a string of words, Fraire would have our whole being walk through them to what is just so. The painter did not paint a mural: he created a world. Master teachers do not deliver a lesson: they deliver a world.

The Apostle John said of his god, "The word became flesh." Master teachers are not gods, but they do strive to do the same with their teachings.

See also

Walking the Path

A Man, a Horse, a Rope

First Lesson

Because I have learned something since last week.

Gandhi, on why he changed his mind

Comment: We have seen filing cabinets full of hanging folders of lesson plans, visual aids, and detailed projects. "Hanging" folder is an apt description. Master teachers do not hang themselves. First lesson: burn last year's lesson. Master teachers begin anew each year because this year's teacher is not last year's teacher. Something new has been learned. And master teachers also acknowledge this year's class is not last year's class. Therefore, last year's ways are not this year's ways. Master teachers also realize today's students are not yesterday's. Students can profoundly change between 2:00 p.m., Thursday, and 7:00 a.m., Friday. Sometimes it is hard to accept this fact. It might mean the lesson plan will have to change.

It happens even faster than that. What is working at the beginning of a lesson might fall apart before the end. Why? Some students are already flowing beyond the lesson while others are caught in a stagnant pool of misunderstanding.

First Lesson

Even faster? We start a sentence, and before the end of it, a student has changed from a smile of comprehension to a frown of befuddlement. Or we start a sentence and memories wash up in their minds—or ours—to create an eddy of ideas and images, sending the academic point in a different direction from the intended flow.

Navigating change is *the* unchangeable challenge of teachers. Heraclites said, "You cannot step into the same river twice." When master teachers address a class, instead of seeing thirty student faces, they see thirty flowing rivers.

They are aware that one flowing river is about to step into another flowing river.

See also

River's Secret

Who Are You?

Dharma Bum Prayer

Equally empty, equally to be loved, equally a coming Buddha.

The Dharma Bums by Jack Kerouac

Comment: Kerouac would place a name in front of this little prayer before saying it. For example: "Michael Jackson. Equally empty, equally to be loved, equally a coming Buddha."

Master teachers find this prayer often liberates them from entangling thoughts when approached by an obstreperous student or an angry colleague. A *Buddha* is anyone who has found enlightenment. The point of the Buddha in the prayer's conclusion is that the student or colleague approaching me *is* me. We are equally on the razor's edge of teaching or life. In fact, we *are* the razor's edge for each other. That is why we have to be careful with one another and recognize who we really are.

See also

Who Are You?

Who Am I?

Greetings

Student: What should I do if I meet Buddha on the path?

Sage: Kill him.

Comment: Ultimately, we do not find any answers outside ourselves. When we read about gifted artists, mathematicians, scientists, and master teachers, we find that their insights, discoveries and successes are organic; that is, they originate from within. Granted, these masters are steeped in the knowledge of others. After all, they are life-long learners. But they also have a talent to take that knowledge and shape it into their own "answers." The gifted become the answer.

So the question is...What should I do if a retiring teacher hands me a file of lesson plans on the Peloponnesian War?

See also

Walk this Way

Boning Knife

Walking the Path

In ancient China, it was common for masters to expect their young students to challenge each other by asking questions that would disentangle the thinking of the other. Here is an example. A student met another walking along a path. The first student challenged: "What are you doing?" The second promptly answered: "I'm walking to the market." The first student went back to his master and reported the exchange. His master reprimanded him for not asking the question: "Why?" The next day, the first student met the second and demanded: "*Why* are you walking to the market?" The second promptly answered: "I'm going to the stream to fill my bucket." The first student returned to his master and reported the answer. The master scratched his head and then sent his student off with a final challenge. The next day the first student met the second walking the path. The first insisted: "The stream is dry. The bucket is broken. What *are* you doing?" The second promptly answered: "I'm walking to the market."

Comment: When a bunch of little kids are sitting cross-legged, suddenly ask them to identify which is their left leg. They will laugh at their own hesitation in answering. The first student on the path thinks he knows his left from his right, but all he can do is pose questions rather than provide answers. However, there is no confusion in the second student's mind. The answer to each challenge is resolute. How can it be any other way? He knows why he is walking the path. The circumstances make it just so. For after all, he cannot walk the path in two different directions at the same time. When truly aware of circumstances, confusion disappears.

There is, however, a cliché in teaching that the question makes the student. There is some truth to that. Yet consider the first student and his so-called master who can only formulate questions, but are befuddled by answers. There are sages who respond to this cliché by suggesting the question is found *in* the answer. Now there is a cross-legged conundrum.

Master teachers relish the challenge of questions and answers. Why? They are not confused. They know their left from the right in learning and life.

See also

Wedding Gift

Walk This Way

Same Old, Same Old

All his life he was prepared to make changes so that things might remain the same.

*****

He drew on the best of the old and new, incorporating novelty without letting it become heresy or anarchy.

How Chief Kamehameha ruled the island of Hawaii. *Shoal of Time* by Gavan Daws

---

Comment: Master teachers recognize the importance of the word *same* in Daws's description of the way Kamehameha ruled his island. The defining qualities of this *same* are wisdom and peace. How clever of Kamehameha to put change in service of the same.

And what about our "kingdom" of education? All the changes, over all the years, in curriculum and methodology should be pointing to that same *same*. The wisdom students gather in school is the same now, as it was in the past, and will be in the future. How we deliver wisdom may change, but wisdom does not. Furthermore, Kamehameha, like a master chef, works with all the ingredients; he does not sacrifice the old just for the sake of the new. What flavors the pot goes in the pot.

Same Old, Same Old

Old or new?— they are all the best. To be sure, master teachers promote and incorporate novelty wherever they can in the classroom, but not to the point of disbelief in the wisdom of learning or "anarchy" in its implementation. Wisdom and peace in education are the same now, as they were in the past, and will be in the future. How we deliver wisdom and peace may change, but wisdom and peace do not.

They are the same old, same old.

See Also

First Lesson

Walking the Path

River's Secret

The river is everywhere at the same time, at the source and the mouth, at the waterfall, at the ferry, at the current, in the ocean and in the mountains, everywhere….

Siddhartha by Hermann Hesse

Comment: This awareness of the river being everywhere at the same time sometimes helps during parent-teacher conferences. The parent expresses great distress over the academic and emotional state of the child, and especially how the child's failings are leading to emotional strife in the home. The parent may even confess wanting to "throw the kid out." At this point the teacher asks the distraught parent: "During your child's early years, did you look forward to the day when—as adults—you would be talking and laughing together at the dinner table?" The answer quite often is *yes*. "Well then?" the teacher wonders. That short "wonder" hopefully will lead to a wistful smile of recognition, longing and re-evaluation of any future actions on the parent's part.

A failed chemistry test, for example, is just part of the flotsam and jetsam of life. But the child who failed the test is not flotsam and jetsam. The child is a river in full flood. The child is six, is sixteen, is sixty—all at the same time. Master teachers understand this "everywhere" in a child's growth… and honor it.

See also

Dharma Bum Prayer

Butcher

Most Valuable Thing in the World

Three young monks sitting in a meditation hall believed they had reached a high level of attainment. Their master posed this question: "What is the most valuable thing in the world?" The first monk opined: "My master's wisdom." The master shook his head. The second offered: "Enlightenment." The master waved him off. The third remained silent. The master thumped him on the head. Later the three monks were sulking in the kitchen and posed the same question to the monastery cook. Without hesitation he answered: "The head of a dead cat."

Comment: Master teachers avoid making judgments about the "value" of students in terms of learning. Students are just so. How do we put a value on the invaluable?

In the middle of a sermon, Buddha halted and said: "Ah, here comes the rain. Let it teach us." Teaching should be like the rain. It falls on the "good" and "bad" alike. Buddha's rain also reminds us that everything is valuable, and being valuable, everything is a potential teaching tool. George Balanchine, the acclaimed director of the New York City Ballet, used to admonish his troupe for not being awake enough to all that might make them good dancers. “We love all things,” he instructed them, “because we need all things.”

But the head of a dead cat? We may believe the head is of no value, but try telling *that* to the distraught owner.

See also

Dharma Bum Prayer

Miracles

A Man, a Horse, a Rope

An uneasy horse. Ray Hunt lays a rope across its neck. They walk out. They walk back. They halt and stand. Together.

Comment: Ray Hunt, the renowned horse trainer, is the teacher. The horse is the student. Okay. But what is the rope? Our first guess might be a brilliant lesson plan or perhaps a particularly effective method of discipline. But what if we look at it this way: Ray Hunt is the rope. Maybe that is his secret. The teacher is the method. Now turn it around the other way: The horse is the rope. In other words, the student is the method. How might that affect taking a class on its walk of learning?

A man, a horse, a rope. But the rope, you see, is not there.

See also

Water Teaching

Greatest Swordsman

Bucket of Water

The king was unhappy. His food no longer delighted him. Time for a new royal cook. All the cooks in the kingdom were summoned to compete for the position. On the day of the contest, the king arrived in his royal park and settled himself comfortably on a pile of goose down pillows. A wooden bucket brimming with cool water was placed before him. To all the aspiring cooks he demanded: "What is this?"

The first contestant stepped forward, dipped his cook's ladle into the cool water, smacked his lips, and announced: "This sweet water will be perfect for my exquisite soups." The king waved him away. A second cook peered into the bucket and announced: "Your Majesty's water is incapable of supporting the complicated structures of my sauces. His Highness will need to fill this bucket with heavy cream instead." The king coughed and sent him off to muck out the royal milking stables. The third cook hesitantly approached, dropped in a sachet, stirred vigorously, and exclaimed: "With this soothing water and my secret recipe, your Royal Highness will taste the excelsior of eternal life." The king scowled and had the charlatan immediately arrested. And so the day dragged on this way, cook after cook.

Late in the afternoon, the king spotted the monastery cook returning from "borrowing" vegetables from the royal garden.

Bucket of Water

"You, there, old monk," the king commanded. "Approach and say what this is." The cook dutifully approached, humbly bowed, and kicked the bucket over.

The king sighed, "If only this old monk cooked for me."

Comment: Here are the textbook guiding questions. Here are the textbook enrichment exercises. Here are the textbook rubrics. Now cook up a successful kid. Textbook adoption committees have faith in this approach to teaching. Of course, teachers appreciate all the help they can get, but should we be handing out the same worksheet, asking the same guiding questions, turning to the same curriculum page on the same day? Master teachers have a different way of cooking. These teachers can take an ordinary textbook exercise and "kick it over" into an extraordinary learning event. Wumen, a Chinese sage, commented: "If I had known the lamp was fire, the rice would have been cooked long ago."

Master teachers discover the fire within the lamp.

See also

Most Valuable Thing in the World

Boning Knife

All Aboard!

Don't worry, I know how to carry it so's it looks light.

Train porter explaining to H.L. Mencken on how he would smuggle the writer's bootleg bottles past prohibition detectives

---

Comment: Class lessons are the bottles. Content knowledge is the weight. The rest is self-explanatory as to how master teachers smuggle challenging ideas past the skeptical minds of students.

See also

Cooking Fish

Wedding Gift

Happy

Vladimir:	Say, I am happy.
Estragon:	I am happy.
Vladimir:	So am I.
Estragon:	So am I.
Vladimir:	We are happy.
Estragon:	We are happy.

Waiting for Godot by Samuel Beckett

Comment: You might try the above dialogue with a student who appears too upset to learn. You play Vladimir. By the end of the exchange, the student will be smiling—reluctantly, perhaps, but smiling.

On the other hand, if tears well up—which does happen—then you are witnessing a truth found in W.H. Auden's poem *The Unknown Citizen*: "Was he free? Was he happy? The question is absurd/ Had anything been wrong we should certainly have heard." The tears are letting us hear. The student feels he *should* be happy, but is frustrated by problems out there. Is there any help to give? Ask the student how he learned to ride a bicycle. "I fell a lot until I got it right" is a likely answer. "But what happened at the moment you got it right?" This question will probably produce a puzzled look. "After falling many times," you helpfully point out, "you turned into the fall. That brought you out of it." Then say: "Turn into it." If you are lucky, you will receive a smile—reluctantly, perhaps, but a smile.

And what about us? Try this at the end of a particularly rough day at school. Turn into it and say: "I'm happy." Not sure it will work? Go ahead, say it now.... There. I bet you smiled—reluctantly, perhaps, but a smile. That smile is a reminder of a truth we intuitively know, but sometimes forget.

Problems are out there. Happiness is in here.

See also

Gravy

Wash Your Plate

Cooking Fish

If you cook a small fish, don't remove its entrails, don't scrape off its scales, and don't stir it. If you do, it will turn to mush.

Ho-Shang Kung

*****

Ruling a large kingdom is like cooking a small fish.

Lao-Tzu

Comment: The lesson plan is the recipe to "cook" the student. Sometimes we get so involved in the recipe that we do not see what is happening to the "fish." The lesson plan is supposed to work this way, so I am going to keep scraping and stirring until every step of the plan has been achieved. The wise authors of *The Joy of Cooking* offer this advice: "A good cook knows through experience how long to cook her fish, but even she will watch the proceedings with a vigilant eye to guard against over doneness." Students know at what point in the proceedings they are being turned to mush. Master teachers know the instant before and turn down the heat.

See also

All Aboard!

Kitchen Cat

Beggar's Wish

A beggar lived in the woods outside the village. His only possessions consisted of a dented cooking pot, a wooden spoon, and a straw sleeping mat. One evening, the beggar was met on the path by a stranger brandishing a knife and demanding his clothes. The beggar hastily removed his shirt and pants and handed them over. The stranger stuffed the clothes in a burlap sack and ran down the path. The beggar then remembered his battered hat. He cried out to the stranger and threw the hat at him. The stranger retrieved it and disappeared into the woods. The beggar smiled at the thought of anyone wanting his old rags.

Now naked, he entered his mud hut to find his few possessions had also been stolen. As he was sitting on the dirt floor and contemplating these amazing events, a thunder storm crashed through the woods. The roof of palm leaves tore away, and through the large opening, the rain poured down on his naked body. Finally, the storm passed, the dark clouds parted, and a silver crescent moon drifted into view. The beggar looked up and sighed:

"If only I could have given him the moon."

Beggar's Wish

Comment: We have all heard this teacher complaint: "I have given everything, but the students still don't get it." In fact, we all have probably proclaimed something similar. We know by now that some students steal all the knowledge they can get; some students need to have it "thrown" at them; and both have been known to cut out before the real gifts arrive.

Lessons are similar to the moon. They have phases: some appreciated for their beauty, some half understood, some missed altogether. Master teachers realize the lesson is only a finger pointing to the moon, not the moon itself. Rather than fret, they patiently smile at the desire and effort to give.

Master teachers accept that they are beggars on the way of learning and strangers to what is really out there.

See also

Smiling Beggar

In the Beginning

Walk This Way

On the sideline of a neighborhood basketball court, two boys were arguing over who was going to be the better power forward for his high school team that winter. The first accused the other of only "talking the talk." The other sneered back: "I walk the talk, man. I walk the talk." The argument was about to become physical when a whistle blew.

The local parish nun, who found her still point in supervising these raucous Saturday morning pick-up games, strolled over and asked what the problem was. The boys bumped chests and spat out the "talk-the-talk" versus "walk-the-talk" argument all over again.

The little nun looked up into the angry faces of these two towering boys, gave them a half-smile, and said: "The two of you can go back on the court when you've learned to *walk the walk*."

Comment: The wisdom of this nun may befuddle the boys, but it is good she is there to help them begin to understand they do not understand. As teachers we want to believe we "walk the talk" because we think we fully understand the "talk." Okay, say we fully

Walk This Way

comprehend the knowledge with all its nuances—a major leap of intellectual faith perhaps bordering on hubris—but in keeping with the boys' argument, say it we will. Now, what does it mean to "walk"? I say the word, but it takes another skill-set so radically different in teaching that it is a miracle some actually accomplish it. And what about those few who transcend both the word and the action? Enter the master teacher. Master teachers are so steeped in their subject knowledge and so sound in its delivery that the classroom questioning and answering come as effortlessly and naturally as walking out the back door to cut flowers for the kitchen table.

In a master teacher's classroom, the student is not there; the teacher is not there; the classroom is not there. So what is there?

Walking the walk.

See also

All Aboard!

A Man, a Horse, a Rope

In the Beginning

This is the real secret of the arts: always be a beginner.

Shunryu Suzuki

*****

For in the place where the beginning is, there the end will be.

Jesus of Nazareth

*****

A movie should have a beginning, a middle and an end, but not necessarily in that order.

Jean Luc Goddard

Comment: Where is the end of the beginning? Where is the beginning of the end? Is there an end? The Principal remarked to a teacher that Grade 8 should be able to write a coherent paragraph. *Mastery*, it is said to be. "Is that so?" the teacher replied and went back to instructing Grade 8 and Grade 9 and Grade 10 on how to write a coherent paragraph. An exercise might just be a beginning for someone in the room. Is that wrong? But even those who are in the middle or near the end will still have to begin again…and again…and again.

In the Beginning

We come across a path in the woods. We step onto it. Are we at the beginning? The end? The middle? There is no order. There is only the beginning we make on it.

There is no end to teaching and learning. There is only the path we are on.

See also

Wisdom

River's Secret

Paradox

An award-winning bull walks through a paddock gate to the pasture. First, its magnificent horns pass through, then its massive chest, now its powerful flanks. But the tail is caught.

Comment: Why is the tail caught? We intuitively know the answer. Nobody is perfect. Just when we are congratulating ourselves on giving the best lesson in the world, a hand of confusion floats up from the back row; or the unit test declares loud and clear that someone does not get it.

Master teachers are just as careful passing through the close of a lesson as they are the beginning. So…if I am careful from the opening to the close in my teaching, then I will frolic in the pasture of student success, right? Master teachers humbly accept the tail will never pass through the gate. In fact, there is no pasture. There is only the gate. Think of all the in-service workshops offering award-winning solutions to our teaching problems. We array ourselves with the latest technologies, methodologies and philosophies and confidently march through the classroom door. Then what happens?

Paradox

See also

Wisdom

In the Beginning

Why Teach?

Disciple: Why teach?

Master: Fill the well with snow!

*****

Disciple: Does a dog have a Buddha-nature?

Master: No!

Comment: Year after year we teach. Does it make any difference? If we answer, *Yes,* we are cut on the razor's edge of self-aggrandizement. If we answer, *No*, we are cut on the razor's edge of false humility. The Buddha dog question speaks directly to this dilemma. According to Thomas Cleary—a master himself of Eastern philosophies—the emphatic *NO* is not the answer to the disciple's question: It is the denial of the question itself. Why teach? Why question it? Master teachers behave like the frog in Basho's haiku:

Old pond
Frog jumps in—
Splash

Sources

Beckett, Samuel. Waiting for Godot. New York: Grove, 1982.

Bolaño, Roberto. The Savage Detectives. Trans. Natasha Wimmer. NewYork: Farrar, 2007.

Cleary, Thomas. Taoist Meditation: Methods for Cultivating a Healthy Mind and Body. Boston: Shambhala, 2000.

Cleary, Thomas, trans. and commentary. Unlocking the Zen Koan. Berkeley: North Atlantic, 1997.

Cleary, Thomas, trans. and ed. Zen Essence: The Science of Freedom. Boston: Shambhala, 2000.

Daws, Gavan. Shoal of Time: A History of the Hawaiian Islands. Hawaii: Hawai'i UP, 1974.

Fields, Rick. How the Swans Came to the Lake, A Narrative History of Buddhism in America. Boulder: Shambhala, 1981.

Hesse, Hermann. Siddartha. Trans. Hilda Rosner. New York: New Directions, 1957.

Hoffmann, Yoel. The Sound of the One Hand, 281 Zen Koans with Answers: Translated with a Commentary. New York: Basic, 1975.

Kabat-Zinn, Jon. Wherever You Go There You Are: Mindfulness Meditation in Everyday Life. NewYork: Hyperion, 1994.

Kerouac, Jack. The Dharma Bums. New York: Viking, 2008.

Layman's Parallel Bible. Grand Rapids: Zondervan, 1973.

Sources

Pine, Red, trans. Lao-tzu's Taoteching. San Francisco: Mercury, 1996.

Rahula, Walpola. What the Buddha Taught. New York: Grove, 1974.

Reps, Paul, and Nyogen Senszaki, trans. and eds. Zen Flesh Zen Bones: A Collection of Zen and Pre-Zen Writings. Boston: Tuttle, 1985.

Rodgers, Marion Elizabeth. Mencken: The American Iconoclast: The Life and Times of the Bad Boys of Baltimore. New York: Oxford, 2005.

Rombauer, Irma, and Marion Rombauer Becker. Joy of Cooking. Indianapolis: Bobbs-Merill, 1967.

Sohl, Robert, and Audrey Carr, eds. The Gospel According to Zen: Beyond the Death of God. New York: New American, 1970.

Suzuki, Shunryu. Zen Is Right Here. Boston: Shambhala, 2007.

---. Zen Mind, Beginner's Mind. New York: Weatherhill, 2001.

Throckmorton, Jr., Burton H., ed. Gospel Parallels: A Comparison of the Synoptic Gospels. Nashville: Thomas Nelson, 1992.

Tricycle: The Buddhist Review. Magazine source of inspiration over the years.

Watts, Alan. The Book. New York: Pantheon, 1966.

---. The Way of Zen. New York: Vintage, 1957.

JOHN GLENNON has taught elementary, middle and high school in California, Wisconsin, Kenya, Burkina Faso, Uganda and Chile. He currently teaches at the American International School of Mozambique. He says he is most definitely *not* a master teacher.

www.ingramcontent.com/pod-product-compliance
Ingram Content Group UK Ltd.
Pitfield, Milton Keynes, MK11 3LW, UK
UKHW041920190726
13854UKWH00003B/1350